Biff, Chip, Wilf and Wilma went to
Holly Blue Fen Nature Reserve.

Sally, the Nature Ranger, met them.
"You can count butterflies," said Sally.

Wilma wanted to see the orchids.
"I'll show you one later," said Sally.

The children counted butterflies.
They ticked the list each time
they saw one.

"I have seen five of the blue ones,"
said Chip. "And three of these."

"We've counted loads of butterflies!" said Wilma. "Can we see the orchids now?"

Sally took them to see one of
the orchids.
"It's been dug up!" she gasped.

Sally was upset. She went off to report the stolen orchid.
"Who would do that?" said Biff.

"What's that man doing?" asked
Chip. "Is he digging something up?"

"He's getting on his bike. Quick!
We must stop him," said Chip.
"I'll run and tell Sally," said Biff.

They raced after the man.
"Don't let him get away!" yelled Wilf.

The children raced as fast as
they could.

"Stop!" called Chip. But the man
didn't stop. He kept going.

Sally ran up the path with Biff.
"Stop!" yelled Wilf.

The man stopped.
"What's going on?" he asked.

"This is Alex," said Sally. "He is a
botanist. He works here."

"Sorry, Alex," said Chip. "We thought you were the orchid thief."

Alex gave a grin.
"Don't worry," he said. "You were
just trying to help."

"What's that lady doing?" asked Chip.
"Don't start that again!" said Wilf.
"She's just looking at the flowers."

"One of the orchids is growing there,"
said Sally. "We'd better check."

"Oh no!" said Sally. "Another orchid has been dug up."

"I bet that woman has stolen them,"
gasped Sally. "We must stop her!"
They all ran after the woman.

Alex took the bag from the woman.
There were the orchids!

"Well done!" said Sally. "We got the orchids back, thanks to you."

"And we got to see them!" said Wilma.